Praise for *Evangeliaries*

"Philip Kolin's *Evangeliaries* is a must-read for those who seriously consider the possibilities inherent in the interaction of the sacred Word with the language and strategies of serious poetry. Again and again, I have found myself caught up in this latest collection of Kolin's lifelong work as a poet, reading and—yes—re-reading the words there on the page, new insights into the deeper inscapes of God's luminous presence, even in darkness, revealing themselves in ever greater abundance."—**PAUL MARIANI**, Distinguished Professor Emeritus at Boston College; author of *Ordinary Time* and *All that Will Be New*

"This beautiful collection draws on the depth and breadth of the Christian life and tradition in a structured series of poems that are not only learned and perceptive but lyrical and accessible as well. Philip C. Kolin's work ponders the miracle of creation, the resonant stories of Old and New Testaments, and the Divine ever-present in history and in our own lives. As a respected scholar, Kolin's knowledge is wonderfully astute; as a skilled poet, his use of word, phrase, and line is deliberate and insightful. But most importantly, as a wise Catholic, Kolin's faith infuses each poem with gravity and grace. From a single uttered 'Amen' to a wealth of 'amended hearts' ('Amen'), *Evangeliaries* is a significant collection, one that instructs and uplifts in equal measure."—**SARAH LAW**, The Open University, London; founder of *Amethyst Review* and Amethyst Press; author of *Therese: Poems*

"Over the course of my life in poetry, I've read several books that transported me to greater understanding, or stunned me with beauty, or brought me to a world hidden in the deep corners of my imagination. But it's rare indeed to find a book that glows with the clarity of white light. Philip Kolin's new collection of poems, *Evangeliaries*, is exactly that kind of rarity. Between the lines of these poems lies a distance spanning from heaven's breath to dirt's redemption, and somewhere en route between alpha and omega we will find ourselves, will find salvation, through this poet's vision. These poems offer that hope page after page, testimony after testimony, from Adam in the garden all the way to three sisters on a Tilt-a-Whirl. But Kolin's poems offer far more than hope. They offer wisdom, faith, truth, and (above all) clarity. For these gifts, for this poet, I am eternally grateful."—**JACK B. BEDELL**, Poet Laureate of Louisiana, 2017–2019; author of *Ghost Forest*

"In the tone of proclaiming the Gospel, the persona in Philip C. Kolin's *Evangeliaries* creates an ambience for readers, not unlike that of participating in the Mass and other liturgical gatherings. Speaking now in declarations, now in imperatives, this voice gifts us with both a sweeping typological vision and a personal plea to holiness; and it does this, not just over the scope of the book as a whole, but in each poem. Individual poems join biblical imagery to liturgical practice in ways that make us reflect deeply, for example, on the physical signs of the Sacraments—water, salt, bread—and wish to make poems like 'Bread' and 'The Host' part of our own personal prayer after receiving the Eucharist. These prayerful 'liturgies' extend from inside to outside traditional worship spaces as well—from the perpetual adoration of the Pink Sisters to the good counsel at a women's shelter to the food trucks of the Capuchins and the pockets of a Walmart shopper who both feed and bless the homeless after being fed themselves by the Gospels; and while in the collection's final pages, we are reminded that those feeding the homeless have been heeding 'the sound advice' of 'the Bible. . . / about estate planning that / will benefit you here and / / in the hereafter,' readers have been prepared for Kolin's teleology from the first poem to the last, when in the opening poem of the collection, we see both the creation of light and 'the perpetual light shining on heaven's saints.'"—**MARY ANN B. MILLER**, Caldwell University; founding editor-in-chief, *Presence Journal*

"In *Evangeliaries*, celebrated poet Philip C. Kolin invites readers on a spiritual pilgrimage through creation, scripture, and the mysteries of our faith. This wonderful collection interweaves the timeless truths of the Gospels with pointed reflections on the human condition.

Using the power of light, fire, and water to offer meditations on grace, charity, and mortality, Kolin's poems also breathe life into both the divine and ordinary aspects of life by drawing on scripture, nature, and sacred tradition. *Evangeliaries* explores the sacred intersections of life, death, and resurrection—guiding the reader from Genesis to Golgotha, from prayer to discipleship, into the hope of eternal life. The author's poetry will inspire readers to slow down to savor the rich spiritual landscapes he unfolds as they journey through Evangeliaries, ultimately reflecting on their own place in the divine story."—**FR. DAVID CONVERTINO**, OFM, Director, St. Anthony's Guild

Evangeliaries

Poems

Evangeliaries

Poems

by
Philip C. Kolin

First published in the USA
by Angelico Press
© Philip C. Kolin 2024

All rights reserved

No part of this book may be reproduced or transmitted,
in any form or by any means, without permission.

For information, address:
Angelico Press
169 Monitor St.
Brooklyn, NY 11222
www.angelicopress.com

pbk: 979-8-89280-060-0
cloth: 979-8-89280-061-7

Cover design: Michael Schrauzer

Acknowledgments

I thank the following journals and presses where earlier versions of these poems have appeared:

Agape: Springtime; In a Walmart Parking Lot

Amethyst Review: Missionaries; Sermons; Epiphany

Assisi: The Towering Ambos in Trees

Blue Collar Review: The Women's Shelter

Blue Unicorn: We Are Awaited

Catholic Prayer Room: Dancing; The Capuchin Food Trucks; Shrouds Don't Have Pockets

Christian Century: Best Said Prayers; Ink; Old Saint Adelbert's Cemetery; Rain on the Pond

Ekstasis: Prayer Warrior Trees; Stars

Ekphrastic Review: *The Angelus*

Green Hills Literary Lantern: The Wisdom of Birds

Gulf Pine Catholic: The Nativity

Integrité: God's Abundance

Louisiana Literature: Monroe's House

Poems for Ephesians: Walking toward Eternity

St. Austin Review: *Ave Maria*; Salt; A Session with a Spiritual Adviser; Stones; Mother Teresa

Thin Places & Sacred Spaces: Three Sisters on a Tilt-A-Whirl

U.S. Catholic: Holy Thursday Pilgrimages; Parables; Water

Valley Voices: Monkey Grass

Windhover: An Old Man Reflects on Job

And I have also included these poems from my chapbook *Wholly God's: Poems* (Wind and Water Press, 2021): Federico, Lazarus Care, On the *Camino Compostela*, The Poor in Spirit, A Woman Who Listened for the Lord.

CONTENTS

Foreword by Joseph Pearce   i

Beginnings

Light   7
God's Breath   8
Stars   9
Angels   10
Fire   12
Water   13
Blessed Dirt   14
Eve   15
Eden   16
Sin   17
Vineyards   18
Gehenna   19

Holy Books & Theological Virtues

The Prophets   23
The Psalms   24
Parables   25
Grace   26
Faith   27
Hope   28
Charity   29

Metaphors & Keys

God's Abundance 33
Bread 34
Sheep 35
Salt 36
Sparrows 37
The Wisdom of Birds 38
Stones 39
Dancing 40
Tares 41
Lepers 42
Bethany 43

Oremus

Ave, Maria 47
The Nativity 48
Epiphany 49
Anna's Prayer 50
The Angelus 51
The Host 52
The Cloister 53
St. Thérèse in the Sacristy Garden 54
Deliver Us from Fear 55
Three Sisters on a Tilt-A-Whirl 56
A Session with a Spiritual Advisor 57
Sermons 58
Praying with God's Second Book 59

Springtide 60
The Towering Ambos in Trees 61
Prayer Warrior Trees 62
Praying the Waves 63
Hallelujah 64
On the *Camino Campostela* 65
Holy Thursday Pilgrimages 68
The Capuchin Food Trucks 67
Discipleship 69
A Woman Who Listened for the Lord 70
The Women's Shelter 71
In a Walmart Parking Lot 72
Mother Teresa 73
Federico 74
The Poor in Spirit 75
Missionaries 76
Unspoken Prayers 77
Amen 78

Life's Last Country
Ink 81
An Old Man Reflects on Job 82
The Last Dwelling of the Flesh 83
Your Last COVID Words 84
Shrouds Don't Have Pockets 85
Rain on the Pond 86
Lazarus Care 87
Old St. Adelbert's Cemetery 89

Walking toward Eternity   90
Monroe's House   91
Monkey Grass   92
We Are Awaited   93

About the Author   94

Foreword

by Joseph Pearce

I have known the author of this volume of poems for many years. I've had the honor and privilege of publishing his splendid verse in the *St. Austin Review* (or *StAR*), the Catholic cultural journal that I've edited since its launch in September 2001, the month of the 9/11 terrorist attacks. Our little "StAR" was, therefore, being born in the literary firmament at an hour in which darkness had descended. In some sense, each of Philip C. Kolin's poems are stars which enlighten the darkness with the light of wisdom and witness.

I will begin this brief foreword with a few words about the wisdom and witness of Philip Kolin, but would like to begin at the very beginning with a definition of terms. This is necessary because poems are only powerful if their potency is perceived. We need to know that when we spell a word we cast a spell. Philip Kolin knows this. His words witness to this. But his readers need to know it too.

Prior to reading the poems on the following pages, it would be good to ensure that we know the meaning of the word "poem," which derives from the ancient Greek and means "a thing that is made or created." A poet is one who makes or creates a thing, and *poiesis* is the act which brings the thing into being. In this original and broadest sense of the word, we can say that God, the Creator, is the primal Poet who brings things into being *ex nihilo*, from nothing. We are lesser or secondary poets who bring things into being from other things that already exist. This is why J.R.R. Tolkien distinguished between God's Creation and human sub-creation.

In the primal sense, we can say that all creatures are poems because they are things made or created. A sunrise is a poem; trees are poems; we are poems. We can also say that the good and beautiful things made by men using the faculty of the creative imagination are poems. A cathedral is a poem; an orchestral score is a poem; a painting is a poem. If we know this, we will know Philip Kolin's poetry; if we don't, we won't.

As for the poems that grace this volume, I am almost afraid to speak of them, mindful of Wordsworth's warning that "we murder to dissect." To pull them apart can do them violence. And yet we must dissect in order to discuss. Doing so without violating the integrity of the work necessitates the critic's pen being wielded with the dexterity of the surgeon's scalpel. Even on the assumption that I had such skill, neither time nor space permits the exercising of it in the limits imposed by a foreword to such a volume. To keep with our medical metaphor, the patient deserves more patience than time and space permits.

Since we don't have the time to single out the individual stars for appraisal (switching metaphors), we will look at the whole galaxy that the volume presents to us and the several constellations within it. As the title suggests, the volume seeks to bring the words and wisdom of the Gospel to enlighten the liturgy of life with God's presence. It begins with *Beginnings*, the *In Principio* of Genesis and St. John's Gospel, the primal things prior to man himself. There are mystical meditations on light, God's breath, stars, angels, fire, and water before we get to the "blessed dirt" from which we were made.

Having started at the very beginning (a very good place to start!), the next constellation in this poetic cosmos, "*Holy Books & Theological Virtues*," takes us deeper into Scripture and virtue. Then comes *Metaphors & Keys* in which the poet perceives what Hopkins would call the inscape of everyday things, such as bread, salt, sparrows and stones, seeing the hand of the Poet in each of these "poems" of his Creation, and seeing them as images or symbols of the Divine and our relationship with it. The largest constellation, entitled "*Oremus*," is devoted to prayer and praise and is itself a prayer in praise of

God's abundance. We see this abundance spilling over in the Presence of Christ in the Eucharist and in the praise of His Mother. We see it in missionaries, in the poor in spirit, and in discipleship; we see it, paradoxically, in unspoken prayers. We see it in diverse and multifarious places, both expected and unexpected. We see it in the cloister but also in the women's shelter; we see it on Holy Thursday pilgrimages but also in a Walmart parking lot. In this ability to see God's abundance in unexpected places, Kolin sings in harmony with Hopkins. God's abundance, His grandeur, shines out. It speaks. It sings. It startles and astonishes.

The final section, the last constellation, is a *memento mori*, a series of meditations on old age and on death, and on what awaits us after death's threshold is crossed. This is as it should be. We should all keep in mind that our life is a pilgrimage. It is a quest for what Hopkins calls the "heaven-haven of the reward." We keep our eye on the finishing line, not because it's the end but because it's the real beginning.

On this note, I'll make my own end.

Those who turn the following pages will be going on a pilgrimage of grace. It is necessary, therefore, to slow down. Poetry, especially poetry this suffused with God's abundant presence, must not be rushed. It must be savored in silence. My advice to those about to go on the following pilgrimage is to give it your entire presence of mind and heart and soul. In doing so, you will be disconnecting from the gadgets that distract us from the quest of life and will be reconnecting with God who is the very purpose of the quest.

Beginnings

"Where were you when I laid the earth's foundation . . . On what were its footings set or who laid the cornerstone. . . Have you ever given orders to the morning . . . [or] comprehended the vast expanse of the east? . . . Do you know the laws of the heavens?"—Job 38

Light

"Let there be light." And so begins
the cosmic geography of Genesis.
"*Fiat lux.*" All else is reflected light.
God's light shone out to the deep dark,
a void lifeless and formless.
Then came the rest of creation.

God made light as essential as breathing.
We could not find our way without it.
Lead on kindly light from expansive
sunlight to the moon's waning crescent.
From sentinels waiting for dawn
to astronomers charting a star's glow.

Light parades in so many ways
and shapes, bands and bows, rays
and ripples, shafts, spots, cascades
and halos, dappled particles and waves.
Holiness enshrined in light keeps us
from spiritual darkness. "*I am*

the light of the world," Christ proclaimed,
true light shining in and through the light.
The light that descended on the Apostles
the first Pentecost. And beyond.

The perpetual light shining on heaven's saints.

God's Breath

Yahweh's name translates into breath
sounds that formed creation out of the void,
galaxies and gardens. He blew life into the dust
that was Adam, implanting in him two praying palms
and a pipe organ in his chest.

Through whirlwinds, whispers, and
tongues of fire, he breathed blessings,
but blasted those evildoers who trespassed
against his sacred name. They returned to dust.

In Bethlehem's body-piercing cold
the Savior cried his name to the world;
but saved his last breath for the Father.

In accord, priests breathe three times on infants
they baptize. At the Chrism Mass, the bishop
breathes on the holy oils. And when the altar
is anointed with incense, we inhale the scent
of eternity. When the body rattles its final breath,
it returns again to the Father whose breath never expires.

Stars

God's diaphanous alphabet to read
bright mysteries hidden behind the clouds.

And when reflected in water mirrors,
they invite encounters with eternity.

Under a wedding canopy of stars,
Adam vespered Yahweh for a twin soul

to share and to console when starlight
left after they ate the forbidden apple.

But God then faithfully seeded Abraham's
generations across the firmament of stars.

And in the fullness of time, the Magi
followed the golden incense of a rising star

as *Christus Oriens* rose in splendor,
a daystar crowned a dogwood cross.

The Virgin's twelve-star halo, Revelation's victory
over those fallen wings, outcasts

from love and worship, dead light nesting
for a third of heaven's hosts.

In the whirr of night, the moon swells
as stars bloom into dahlias and zephyr lilies.

Angels

They wear air but do not breathe it,
yet they have a multitude of eyes wheeling

around and two wings to shield their sight
from God's radiant countenance.

Countless, they circle every altar; size or number,
only measures of our frail world; eternity is limitless.

They wear jewelry of fire and polished
beryl; and golden belts from Uphaz;

and glimmer in a rainbow of colors—
from Marian Blue to celadon to coral rose.

Unseen spirits, they don human faces
and costumes when as messengers

delivering birth announcements—
to Abraham at the terebinth of Mamre,

to a speechless, doubting Zechariah,
and to the Virgin at her prie-dieu.

Evening angels entered dreams
warning Joseph that the child

is heaven's gift and telling the Magi to travel
home by another way, avoiding Herod.

Comforters and healers, angels cradled Jesus
in the starving desert and at Gethsemane.

The Archangel Raphael, often called
beside a sick bed, cured Tobit with fish gall.

And the fierce warrior Michael protects us
from prowling demons and their snares

as our guardian angels keep watch over us
throughout the entrapping night.

Fire

God's eyes blazed as he speaks in tongues of fire.
He brandished his fiery sword and is surrounded
by fire angels, the Seraphim. His altar remains

afire forever; he refines his disciples
like gold in a furnace. But destroys sinful
cities with rains of fire and sulfur.

He built Gehenna's burning pit for those fallen
principalities, forever wasting away in that dark inferno.
God's fire tests us as witness Shadrach,

Meshach, and Abednego's faithfulness.
Or when, smoldering wicks that we are,
we beg him to relume us. Souls powerfully slain

in the Spirit are baptized with holy fire.
But sometimes fire speaks gently, as in Lent, when
wax-weeping candles accompany our prayers,

or at the Easter Vigil when the fire from
the Paschal candle multiplies to flame each
parishioner's taper, spreading *Lumen Christi*.

Water

We are flesh made for water, bone and soul.
Our thirst cries out, gritty voices longing for
still waters, the promise of rescue.

Delivering the remnant from the gnashing flood,
drenching the Nile with frogs, and parting
the Red Sea swallowing Pharaoh,

God then instructed Moses to rod-strike a rock
quickening it into water, washing Naaman's leprosy
away, and splitting the Jordan so Joshua
and the Twelve could enter the promised land.

Jesus stilled the harrowing storm, walking
on the Galilee, and filling parched ears
with parables delivered from a rippling boat.

Holy acts are sealed with water.
Baptisms, Siloam healings, Eastertide
aspergings; calming rains from a cloud canopy
refreshing us like sunflowers; showers and dewfall
greening the countryside with the blessings
of the harvest; pools and ponds reflecting
heaven's nightly buoys, the stars.

Our lives are written in water. The womb's sea
brings us into the world and holy water sprinkled
over our grave carries us out, out into the deep.

Blessed Dirt

Not all dirt is snake-slimed or sin-cursed.
God called us from dirt and dirt is what calls
us back to him. Adam was aptly named for red dirt.
And God blessed Isaac whose sower's seeds

glowed in fields ripe with feasts and flowers.
God declared the soil holy when he ordered Moses
to remove his shoes when standing before him.
The clouds themselves likened to the dust

God walks on in the heavens. The ashes we receive
in Lent are dust purified, the cloak of our humility
before God. "*I am dust and ashes*," cried
Father Abraham, and King David sprinkled ashes

on his bread, repenting his lust. Nineveh
heaped itself in ashes seeking God's forgiveness.
And on the last day our dust will rise
as we ascend to the ash-spackled stars.

Eve

Because it was not good for man
to be alone amid all this plenty
God gave him a wife taken from
his rib cage, the bone closest to his heart.

Under one of Eden's flourishing boughs
Eve began her beginning swathed by
God's honeysuckle breath.
She wore wildflowers in her hair
and ran through Eden like a gazelle.

When she named the animals,
they did not make the same sounds back.
But she and Adam enjoyed the laughter
in God's voice and in each other's.

Her body dreamt only of yesterdays
except one night she saw large yellow
stars and crosses burning and crying out,
yet she had no memory of who or what they were.

She was Eden's first lady, born to be
reborn, a mother to generations forever.
Her blood ran like a nourishing river
and her womb grew as large as an orchard
watered by tears.

Eden

Encircled by angels
this garden of delight
fragranced by God's voice.

Trees, vines, bushes
fair to the sight and taste;
pomegranates without thorns

or taint of sin except
that one tree filled with grace
unless touched.

Adam surrounded by liquid
pearl at moonrise, a time for cleaving
to a mate for an abundance of time

naming God's creation and
frolicking in hail holy
wedded love.

Then Eve tending a serpent's trick
shared sin with her mate;
and the two became shame-attired.

God's stern voice, a prophecy now—
disobedience brings death; Eden's gates
shut. Angels encircled Eden.

Sin

Breaking away from God.
Cultivating darkness, denying light.

Pinnacling self over everyone
and everything; gossip mongering;

twisting someone's wedding ring
off; setting brother against brother.

Stuffing your conscience daily
with easy denials or tempting pleasures;

imploding with wrath; spreading despair;
grinding your heart into stone. Following

the call of the world's vanities—
titles, awards, wealth, land, filthy rags.

Giving wily-handed, and soul-deadening pride
the rope to hang you.

Vineyards

God's kingdom planted in Israel,
a vineyard of promises where souls like seeds
ripened by the sun, refreshed by rainclouds.

A winepress recorded generations multiplying
their labor and prayers for a green and
generous harvest. A watchtower broadcast

if an enemy lurked, and a fortress hedge
and staunch stone fence encircled
this hallowed ground.

But hired sinners rebelled against
the owner's covenants and slew his son
and faithful followers. Blight then struck row

after row. A menagerie of ruin let loose—
blackbirds with trampling beaks and crafty
fox with bitter teeth bit grapes sour with sin.

Unfenced and untended, the vineyard then
was invaded by briers, thorns, cockles,
nettles and fescue; wine turned to weeds.

The unfaithful plotters had their inheritance
doled out in shrieks. And the fruit of the vine
was not drunk again until the heir entered paradise.

Gehenna

Terror is its history. A burning altar
with children's flesh and cries
for a Tophet of cruelty. Then
Jerusalem's garbage dump
stenched with offal, the dreck of
putrefying cadavers.

Now Christ's burn pit for sinners' souls,
traducers with lusty eyes, hands
that bullied and stole, mouths that spit
raqa at their enemies, blasphemers
cursing Yahweh and his covenants.

Forever removed from the holy city
with its temple bells, walls, and cracks
for prayers. Sparrows never fly here;
wandering clouds turn to dust.
The fires never slack.

No one dies here just once;
they die a second death each day.

Holy Books & Theological Virtues

"Through the prophets God forms his people in the hope of salvation in the expectation of a new and everlasting covenant intended for all to be written on their hearts."
—*Catechism of the Catholic Church* 64

"We ought to pray all 150 Psalms at least once a week."
—St. Benedict

"These virtues are called theological first because their object is God, inasmuch as they direct us aright to God."
—St. Thomas Aquinas

The Prophets

Eighteen messengers crying out for the Lord.
Oracles, mystics, seers, poets
infused with ecstasy. Unbound from

the world's decrees, they heard
God's voice as a roaring river or
a passing whisper.

Their words inscribed in visions.
"*I saw the Lord,*" proclaims Isaiah. "*He is high
and lifted up,*" Ezikiel wrote of his blazing visions

while Daniel predicted the destruction of
the temple; and Micah dreamt that without
a leader, the chosen people were lost sheep.

Prophets warned of the coming of God's Great Day.
Of injustices punished; smitten for following
false gods. Obadiah foretold the fall of Edom

and Haggai called out those who lived
in plush-paneled houses while God's Ark
dwelt in ruins.

But the prophets seeded hope and God's mercy, too.
"*Return to me with your heart, and I will
return to you,*" promised Yahweh.

Hosea told of God's sorrow for his people: "*All his
compassion is awakened.*" And seeing the Christ,
the last of the prophets John testified to the light.

These holy men looked forward to Bethlehem,
Golgotha, and the New Jerusalem
where the Lord abides.

The Psalms

Sacred songs that praise, plead, and confess to God.
Trumpet blasts, the clash of cymbals, the ram's horn
calling. Let the festal chorus magnify God's fullness.
Trees watered by fresh springs; meadows cloaked
with flocks. Harvests grow rich and fish fill the seas.

Honor God in the stronghold of his sanctuary.
He surrounds us with cloud-capped mountain peaks
as he does in Jerusalem. We hear him in the thunder-
crashing waves and as he quiets the winds
down to a hush. Yet his mighty voice breaks
cedars and flashes fire. We come under his wing

for protection from the fowler's net. He rebukes
workers of evil with their flattering lips and lewd
eyes that swell with fat. Their throats are like
open graves. He confounds their speech and
makes them vanish like smoke.

These Psalms talk to God who hears our pain flowing out
like blood in battle. But when we sin, we tremble
at his anger and ask why he hides his face.
Still he comforts us when we have strayed and calls
his lost sheep home again.

Parables

Ears to see, eyes to hear the secrets
of the Kingdom. Shine before others.
Trim your lamps; be a light on a hilltop; scatter
seeds, but guard against choking thorns, poaching
birds, hungry rocks; an enemy's weeds.

Be yeast and multiply. Open your doors
at midnight. Balm the wanderer's wounds.
Pour new wine into new wineskins.
Dig up hidden treasure.
Look for pearls worth a great price.
Earn interest on your God-given talents.
Verdict in favor of the widow. Pay a full denarius
for a half day's work.

Lost coin. Lost sheep. A lost son,
feeding on pig pods, come home now
to his longing father gifting him
with a robe, a ring, a fatted calf.
Avoid enlarging the sawdust speck
in your elder brother's eye while ignoring
the plank in yours.

Barns, barns, barns; a rich fool's unaware last hour.
The Pharisee tithing his pride; the lowered
eyes of a repentant tax collector.
The gluttony of Dives's purple; a beggar's sores
healed in Abraham's bosom.

The harvest has come. *Amen.*
Wear wedding clothes. Sit higher
or lower depending on where you are called.
Savor those words which will never pass away.

Grace

God's gift, unexpected, unmerited,
unmatched; flush with faith, favor,
fervor, forgiveness, leading us out
of captivity. Restoring song to our lips.

Christ's tree redeeming Adam's
with eternal promise. The love
that never leaves us, that takes the crucified
down daily from crosses of cruelty.

Grace, too, in the bounty of the Pink Sisters'
prayers around the clock and throughout the calendar
interceding for our frail-voiced intentions.
Unbounded riches for our soul's protection.

It lets us know we are cherished—
saved from the fowler's coiled net and
the prowler's wily grasp. It is oil brimming
over for those dark nights of the soul.

God's grace waits in a smile, a yes, a rainbow,
a hymn, a cardinal warbling in the morning.

Faith

A garden full of mustard seeds,
St. Thérèse's "Little Way" to heaven.
Dame Julian singing, *All will be well; All will be well*
from her beehive cell in that Norwich church.
Catherine of Siena kept alive
by taking no food but only Holy Communion.
St. Hildegard whirling in God-spanned
visions of the universe.

Reverence also the martyr's buckler, losing
bodies as their souls ignite. St. Joan comforted
as her body burned; St. Lucy's plucked
eyes seeing Christ; Fr. Jogues holding up
the chalice, his fingers gone.
His body thrown into the Mohawk River.
The heads of those 21 Coptic Christians
toppling to the ground in Libya, but each wearing
a glowing nimbus in heaven.

Honor contemplative souls as well hearing God
speak about himself directly to them.
Aquinas penning his encyclopedic *Summa* day after
day. St. Anthony holding the Christ Child
in his arms. St. Peter Alcantara scribing in his carrel,
the Holy Spirit fluttering inspiration above. St. Faustina
keeping her diary as the Father tells her what to write
and how to paint that image of Mercy flowing with
rays of red and blue. Faith scattering darkness.

Faith is announced, too, in fish drawn on ancient
catacomb walls; and in graveyards limned with crosses.
And in rainbows rising high and higher above mountains
thrown into the sea.

Hope

It's the blessing with wings. Noah's
eventide dove landing ahead.
Swallows bringing spring back
to Capistrano; canaries caroling
to miners; the pelican feeding all
those at the Communion rail.

And it is anchors, too, safeguarding
those fallen asleep. These holy signs
embedded in catacomb walls and imprinted
on early tombs steadfasting the saints
in heaven. It's also the missionary's emblem—
the anchor cross—sealed on hopeful breasts.

It's in the promise made to Abraham
that his descendants would outnumber
the stars; and that the roadmap in *Exodus*
would lead God's chosen to the promised land.
And that the infant old Simeon held would save Israel.
It assured Paul that his blindness on the road to Damascus
would bring him into the light.

It is seeing what is not there. And yet is.

Charity

She is a mother, patient and giving, overflowing
with children, breastfeeding one, rocking
another at her side, all the while helping several others climb
the folds of her robe to reach her bountiful heart.

She stands above the high altar at St. Louis Cathedral
with her sisters Faith and Hope. At times she is painted
holding a chalice with the Eucharist blazing above it,
her face glowing with the glory of sacrifice.
Where she is, there is Christ. Love creating love.

She has taught us to be Corinthians—
to feed the hungry by planting generous fields,
to love the unloved by nurturing the stranger,
to spend words lavishly on prayers, and to celebrate
the fullness of creation.

We are her children.

Metaphors & Keys

"I will instruct you and teach you in the way you should go; I will counsel you with my eye upon you."—Psalm 32:8

"Metaphors have a surplus of meaning; they are texts in miniature."—Paul Ricoeur

God's Abundance

God feeds his people manna
in the midst of a desert of emptiness;
and after this hoarfrost harvest,

quail. Then loaves of spelt and millet,
lentils and barley, sun dripping with
crescent richness for his earth-fed flock

that followed a calendar
with an abundance of days
in spite of the changing
space they had to plant and pray.

At last the Seder that welcomed
the Savior who feasted apostles
and all their descendants
on the bounty of his flesh.

Bread

"I am the bread of life." —John 6:35

Down long aisles to the altar with bent
heads, we open our mouths to receive
mystery: this bread we consume

now consumes us. Under our roof
this bright host brings a transfiguration.
In every particle Christ enters, putting on

the flesh that covers us as Spirit becomes
substance. In the dark wood of our pews
we hold him as he beholds us from the cross

inside us. Speaking balm-filled words,
he pleads with us to forgive those whom
we have scourged with cold distance

or who have planted thorns in our hearts.
He tells us his body carries the blistering
hurts we have suffered.

But how blessed we are that
like the Apostles the risen Christ
miraculously comes into

our upper room, standing
in our midst, breaking his bread
of sacrifice with us.

Sheep

Woolly clouds with cloven feet:
heaven and earth outnumbering
all other animals in Holy Writ.
God's people thirsting for direction
and defense, survival and salvation.

Woe betide wicked shepherds who fail
to water, care, and cure their flocks,
leaving them to scatter on the mountains,
prey for ravenous beasts, refusing
to search for the lost sheep as night descends.

Follow those good shepherds, God's anointed:
Joseph, Abraham, Moses, David, Rachel,
and Peter who showed such kindness
to their sheep. "*I am the Lamb of God*,"
Jesus told them, the one who takes away

"*the sins of the world*," the sacrifice
paid for our transgressions, the cost of
one temple lamb. Reflect on those shepherds
from Bethlehem witnessing the Christ,
the infant king and Lamb of God.

He is also the Good Shepherd who knows his sheep
as they know his voice; he is the door opening
the sheepfold, pointing to their sanctuary.
Script and Scripture, the Holy Word writ on sheep
skin parchment, shared, savored, and celebrated.

Salt

Harvest salt, an ocean's, a mine's,
salvation's worth. Extract it from tears.

Salt is the soul's seasoning that seals
the covenant between Adonai and Adam.

Pour it over your offerings. Add it
to the incense that sanctifies your praise.

Rub your newborns with it, passing
these holy ones among the congregation.

Let it preserve your bonds
with others, a soul-sturdy contract.

Keep it clear as rock crystal, and
never let it stale in the darkness.

May it be the light within you
as you journey to the mountaintop.

Sparrows

Five sparrows for two pennies. Counted
expendable, they have caught God's eye.

Summoned to temple altars as consecrated
sacrifices, they exchanged their wings

for incense swirling up to heaven.
They live among fields and vineyards
and build nests in trees and around the eaves
of houses. They sing on rooftops.

Pilgrims with feathers, they call us
to humility and gentleness; clouds
of witnesses notating the air and
providing winged manna and hope

for the poor. St. Hildegard prophesied
that the Word manifests itself in every
living creature. We and these sparrows
are joined in God's Book of Creation.

A twelve-week-old womb baby weighs
about a half ounce. That's approximately
the same as a very young sparrow, and both
under God's watchful eye.

The Wisdom of Birds

A sand dove nested
in a pomegranate tree

her high-pitched coos
instructing her brood.

A cardinal swooping
down snatching

infernal wasps
while policing the skies.

A band of sparrows
chirping Matins

consoling the late
autumn air.

Stones

"I tell you that if these remain silent, even the stones will cry out." —Luke 19:40

Carry stones in your shepherd's sack
on your pilgrimage. Hear in them
the voices of holy history: those *Hosannas*

across palm-strewn paths; the women
keening over their barren wombs. The thudding
steps of two men, the blood of one soaking

into the stones, his face cambered
in Veronica's shroud. Peter's guilty tears
as heavy as limestone moaning

as it is crushed down by the weight
of the wood. All nature outraged
by the journey these stones must bear.

Anchored in blood and Golgotha's
cruel rock, the cross bewailed by prophets
from Isaiah to Malachi rises.

Hear the harrowing of the stone
rolled back from the borrowed tomb
in the ash-scented garden and behold

the angel standing in the slant
light of morning—the emptiness of the tomb,
the fulfillment of time.

Dancing

"You have turned my wailing into dancing."
—Psalm 30:11

God first danced the spheres into music
and called Judah back with pipe and timbrels.
Women danced together; men danced together
in one great feast of forgiveness.

Prophet Mariam leapt as Pharaoh's chariots
and riders were swallowed by the Red Sea.
But as Moses was praying atop Mount Sinai,
below his people gamboled before a golden calf.

In thanks David danced naked in his linen apron
before the returned Ark, God's choreographer.
While Salome slithered to a tabor, firing Antipas's lust,
dropping one veil, then others to the floor.

At Cana Jesus danced among the men and filled
six stone jars swaying with wine on the third day.
Hearing music afar off, the prodigal returned,
a calf (not golden), rings and robes waiting.

And the Father danced.

Tares
St. Matthew 13:24–30

Dressed in darnel and chaff, they flourish
in the dark air. Tares, rooted in Satan,
yield toxic black bread when the blessed grain

is plucked with them. Beware these look-alike
green spies in the fields of your soul
who will betray your fruitful harvest.

They are false prophets garnering followers
to feed them heresy and trample their faith.
Do not load your storehouse

with unholy plants. Plans for good deeds
unspent preach selfishness in the end, so
search seeds before you plant them.

Soil has a keen memory of what it births
and cannot lie to the harvest master or his
angel reapers who will bundle up

false grain from the threshing floor
and burn all the darnel and chaff
in everlasting fire.

Lepers

Untouchables, exiles from love, they lived
outside the camps; even families could not see
them behind the rocks where they hid.

Fleas and flies feared landing on one
of them, scabrous ridden and muffled.
Leviticus unhesitatingly consigned them

among the living dead. If anyone dared
approach, they had to stay back
fifty paces and double that if the wind blew.

Their disease was sin-borne, and every sore
an offense against the purity laws. The priests
placed thorn bushes around lepers

to keep their souls away from the tabernacle and
the temple preventing the contamination of
officials and worshippers there. But when Christ

touched a leper, he became one of them, an outcast
taking refuge in lonely places and then suffering
on the cross with all those lance and nail wounds.

Bethany

The house of God, city of figs, a sacred mount,
on Jordan's eastern bank, Christ's baptism;
half a mile to an untethered colt, two to Jerusalem,
a blood-soaked furlong more to Golgotha.

Sabbath feasting at a leper's; cleansing caustic skin;
Lazarus's sisters, one troubled with household chores;
the other with the better part, listening, pouring
precious spikenard from an alabaster jar

anointing the young rabbi as if for burial;
drying his feet lovingly with her long, free flowing hair.
Lazarus gone into in a dark sleep behind a rock;
Mary searching the roads for the master—
four days until he arrives.

Then Christ's tears blossoming into lilies, and Lazarus,
still bound, emerging from his tomb, the stench supplanted
by the scent of nard rushing throughout the city.

Christ's last week here; six days from a dogwood tree;
then three more, another stone rolled back,
another resurrection; forty more, the ascent from
the Olive Mount into the clouds, the house of God.

Oremus

"Prayer makes us brothers and sisters."—Pope Francis

"Ora et labora."—St. Benedict

Ave, Maria
   Luke 1:46–55

So young to fulfill ancient prophecies.
The herald of heaven's joy woos her
in courtier Aramaic. His words jasper-like;
his face aglow; a lily in his hand.

A prayer from Isaiah hangs on
her lintel; butterflies fill the sky.
Be it done unto me. In her dreams she sees
temple flocks and doves and is overshadowed

as heaven enters her womb; carrying the heir
of the Ark—a child with manna, a high priest,
a man of sorrows. *My soul doth magnify the Lord.*
She is his tabernacle, that sacred space
on altars across time

where her son feeds the world. Still,
what of that terrifying prophecy proclaimed
by that righteous old man in the temple that
her heart would be pierced as she climbed

the Via Dolorosa with her thorn-crowned son,
his blood soaking the steps leading the way.
Then crushing the head of that seraph serpent,
once an archangel, forever the archenemy.

August fields today proclaim her through overflowing
harvests and healing herbs. Campaniles ring out *"Aves,"*
again and again, celebrating the maiden chosen
by the Father to give his son flesh.

The Nativity

In the keep of the world's misery, when
the time before came balanced against
the time to come, a child created the light

that sceptered the darkness with stars.
His birth became the apex of hosts,
unseen choirs released from sacred silence.

A congregation of temple sheep,
whose feet dare not touch the earth,
gathered to homage heaven's daystar.

Infinity was caressed then by eyes humbled
yet with voices lifted on high,
holy as notes from chapel organs.

Epiphany

A star gives directions to find a child who brings light on this dark and cold night

His cries contain all the prayers ever said.

God has saved them for just this hour when miracles outdistance time

Anna's Prayer

"There was also a prophetess, Anna . . . eighty-four years old. She never left the temple, but worshiped night and day with fasting and prayer. And coming forward at that very time, she gave thanks to God and spoke about the child to all who were awaiting the redemption of Jerusalem."—Luke 2:36–38

I saw her, slight, young, luminous eyes,
come to deliver that baby swaddled like a temple lamb
to the Lord, whom I have served so long in this sacred place.
Even when I was young I heard whispers about this moment.
My prophecy was my gift to her.

The husband's hands were sewn with callouses
and his face hewn out of wailing stones.
But his eyes shone like golden candles,
and his tallit blazed brilliant green.

That day turtledoves escaped their coops
and took to the air like clouds given wings,
and coming back they looked like pieces
of heaven's canopy falling to earth.
The temple was filled with a light I had
never seen before, enrapturing my soul.

In the Savior's soft cries, I heard tearful *Hosannas*.

The Angelus
After Jean-Francois Millet's 1859 painting "The Angelus"

Three times a day the bells remind the air
that eternity is not that far away
and that flesh has found its fulfillment.

Dawn rings with God's promise to all—
the incarnation of the sun
heralded in the fullness of the bells.

At midday the bells tell of an angel's bowing
before a lustrous handmaiden confirming
heaven's radiance come into a soiled world.

Dusk lingers until the last chorus of the bells
sounds jubilation at Mary's *Magnificat*—
Christ dwelling among us as day's work is done.

The Host

God's glory conveyed in one syllable—*host*—
opening a litany of praise.

He is the *hostia*, the victim who atones for our crimes,
the sacrificial lamb, the blood over
the doorways of our lives, the slain Savior—
then, now, forever.

He is also both the guest and the holy welcome,
the *hospes* and the *hospitis*.

With our hands and our tongues
we welcome this visitor to sojourn in our souls,
the flesh and the feast, the *hostel*,
God who empties himself
into us.

This one-syllable gift of love
is bestowed on us
no matter what we may be—
hostage or *hospitalier*.

The Cloister

Within the hidden architecture of the cloister
God calls through carrels and cells; his silence
circulates like incense; the air tastes like prayers.
Walls and gates stop the world from pushing in.

Grilles have a thousand eyelets to peer out,
yet the nuns' vision goes beyond what their eyes see.
They have forsaken hectic 24-hour time,
and live according to the seven holy hours.

Twelve thin beds wait for brides in vow-thick wool;
no dressers or closets, only temptations to gather
worldliness. Since bodies do not ascend,
their former selves are sealed in an ossuary.

They hear the sacred speaking through
small icons—thorns, pearls, sparrows, lost
drachmas, doves, mites, mustard seeds.

A blessing for over a century and a half,
but today the long arms of steely cranes
and rowdy bulldozers brawl
to break the silence of this house.

Glory still rises from the dust.

St. Thérèse in the Sacristy Garden

*From a photo taken in 1896 at Lisieux by Céline,
also a Carmelite nun and St. Thérèse's own sister*

Twenty-three now and seven years professed,
she holds a lily in the sacristy garden, enclosed
like herself, here where Christ dwells.

Cloaked in white over her scapular and beneath
that the rough wool of a nun's brown tunic.
She is sealed now to the Christ whose cross

shimmers behind her in the Carmel underbrush.
Christ is her divine spouse and she welcomes
every cross that comes to her. On Good Friday

she had her first TB hemorrhage. She is his
Psalm 85, a prayer inscribed in flowers. She means
to fling sweet petals before his cross from heaven's bowers

and scatter roses to save sinners on earth. This will be
her mission, once her lungs and heart are riven.
But for now this single lily blooms as her bridal bouquet.

Deliver Us from Fear

"Fear is love's opposite . . . When we consult love instead of fear, our innocence and goodness catch up with us."
—Gregory Boyle, S.J., The Whole Language

Fear cries out in panic, screams, and shrieks.
Being caught, trapped, doomed;
besieged by the terrors of the night.
The enemy strings arrows to murder sleep.

A knock on a sharecropper's cabin
at midnight; dogs howling,
a blasphemous cross blazing in a yard;
the smell of tar invades the air. Swastika armed
bands search for gold stars to put out.
A deadly pestilence stalks

as soul assassins spew poison
to sicken your hope but, worse yet,
to infect your faith and enslave your soul.
They plot to throw you into the deep valley

of shadows where ten thousand fall daily
and there, among gnashing and wailing,
devour you in fire that darkness never dims.

But neither depths nor demons can snatch
us away from God's deliverance and love.
Seal his words on your lips to frighten the devil away.

Make Christ your hiding place.

Three Sisters on a Tilt-A-Whirl

St. Pius Carnival, Chicago, August, 1955.
Three wimpled sisters board a Tilt-
A-Whirl ride, a half shell spinning,

bouncing, fluttering their habits and
blurring the faces of bystanders, melting
gaudy lights, and whirling them beyond

a blocked-off carnival street—
caught up in the clouds at last to meet
their Lord in the air.

Dizzy to the point of ecstasy, the sisters
feel a rush of laughter; their prayer language
on this ride like that of the mystics' centuries-

long jubilation at their marriage to the Lamb.
The Tilt-A-Whirl has become their prayer cell;
God come to them in festive fury

so unlike the starched views of him
they were taught and had been teaching.
And now, as the ride ends, their limbs

have grown so much lighter.
Must they confess this to Mother Superior
as they return to their bodies.

A Session with a Spiritual Adviser

We stir with silence as we sit opposite
each other on strict wooden chairs.
She offers me a glass of barley water
and then gives me this holy counsel:

"Let God have a good look at you. How much
poverty have you acquired since we last met?
Continue to strip yourself from your possessions.
To be poor is to be free. Obey Mother Teresa.
Disown your closets. Embrace emptiness.

Replace parrot prayers mumbled without
sacrifice with mendicant thanksgiving.
Be like the Desert Fathers whose syntax
was not mired in tenses and inflections.
Verbs implying we have the power to move

or to be were anathema to them. God's grammar
reverberates in silence. Adopt the righteousness
of tress that won Jacob's blessing for their courage.
Though wordless they still have voices. Rooted
in earth, they climb for the stars. Breathe in
their inspiration. Listen for their *Hallelujahs*.

Our session is done. Go into the night
and wait for visions."

Sermons

The preacher's words winnow the air.
Pray with your eyes closed. Listen to
God singing. Be grateful for birds and breezes.

Humility means never carrying an umbrella.
Storms are temporary; sunshine is inevitable.
Don't let grudges worm into your heart.

Live on the heavenly side of your life.
When angels come, they come with seeds
in their pockets, not money. Time vanishes

in eternity. Tombstones are only memories
of souls passed. When Jesus descends to judge,
he will speak just one word to each of us—
More? or *Less*?

Praying with God's Second Book

Go to churches in brawny forests,
under a pied sky, or on a craggy beach.
Be dazzled by darting minnows, those cherubim of the sea.
Hear hymnals in the wind; angel wings whispering
in the mists and mallow breezes.
All proclaiming the redemption of green
in knolls and prairies, savannahs and steppes.
Taste God's blessing from honey bees
swarming in raptured air.

But sorrow, too, for fields blighted pesticide white,
the lamentation of the loons and chaparral.
Still accept indulgences as well in the late afternoon sun.
Clouds, scrubbed now, caressed with the Spirit's calming pastels.
Applaud caterpillars morphing into butterflies.
The full moon calls us to Compline, prayers crying out
in the dark. See lambs and fish as holy greeters
at heaven's gates as God's Second Book readies
for dawn readings.

Springtide

The earth hidden in darkness aspires
now toward the glories of renewal.
Not with drumrolls or clapping clouds
but in the unseen silence of taproots
gathering sweetness underground.

Now starts the season of soft color, azaleas
cladding themselves in lithe purple and
announcing the good news about
the lengthening and warming of a gentle sun.
For too long a brown monotone warped hope

but now surrenders to the lush quiet of verdant shoots
sprawling across every place not censured
by dull cement. The world that wailed
in pelting chill these last bleak months
hallowed now by the florescence of spring.

The Towering Ambos in Trees

With their massive outstretched arms
they preach the wisdom of green
recovering after the forest's fullness

fell, a graveyard of embalmed brown
and pockmarked snow; stinging sleet
winging through bare boughs.

From their towering ambos of elm,
spruce, maple, and oak once more
they teach about the sacrifice of loss

and bountiful resurrection, a cadence
of light and breath, seed and root,
blooming now in unpent leaves, star-

gazing flowers, fragrant golden fruit,
reminding us that we too live inside
the yew, the pine, the raintree, the ash.

They entreat us to hold as much spring
as we can awakening from our own
withering winter season.

Prayer Warrior Trees

They weave papyrus-like hymns
in the language of leaves
about the dazzling seasons delivering
love letters to the sun. Or wrinkled, send
requiems down to the crisping soil.

But their limbs can also push
aside cables and wires as well as
impart prayers to the heavens
in moonlit strokes on blackboard skies,
pleas for solace after a storm.

They also choreograph the wind's
wonders, soughing or bristling,
or can be still as a pond in January.

They convene choirs for Matins
and Vespers in nature's cathedrals.

Praying the Waves

The waves in the Gulf rush
as if the Spirit were brooding over
these waters, deep calling to deep.

In each wave I hear a voice
from their curled lips rolling in jubilation—
so high they seem to touch heaven.
Still, I cannot see through them,

though they see through me,
a beachcomber sifting for faces
buried at sea or in the wake of
a boat churning.

I reflect on the fishermen calling out
to Christ as he walked on Galilee's waves
that tested Peter's frightened faith
and mine, too, as I sit safely

here on the shore. And the waves keep
rushing in as if wrapped in parchment
scrolls asking me to heed the messages
that brought peace to the Galilee fishermen.

Hallelujah

Hallelujah—what a powerful prayer word.
Syllables of joy and praise clinging
to Yahweh's earth-shortened name.

This word, spoken, sung, or played on
trumpets or harps, declares the promise
of bliss at being created by

the maker of the universe. Every atom
from the world of seeds to the spinning
planets brings us out of darkness

and into God's stirring light. Saying the word
invites us to give ourselves to prayer by ourselves
or as part of a quorum.

It's as if God himself is indwelling
between our lips teaching our souls
how to be holy. *Hallelujah*.

On the *Camino Compostela*

From Roncesvalles to Galicia all creation walks west
following the Basque sun which ends in the shadowy
light of the saint who was also an apostle.

For a thousand years, pilgrims have followed him
across streams, through tunnels, over jagged peaks
and down rock-sown slopes.

God bruises pilgrim heels so they do not walk
after flesh but toward the Spirit. Put some stones
in your backpacks, beads for a Pyrenees rosary.

A heavy blessing. But along the journey flowers
burst into bloom and we are serenaded
by crested larks, Alpine swifts, red-billed choughs.

And yet the world's beauty is rooted in suffering.
We carry scallops and a small portion of bread—
a hostel's communion of friendship.

There is talk of miracles ahead. At night
each pilgrim becomes a flickering votive candle,
a bright prayer in the silence of the *Camino* shrines.

In the alphabet of Calvary, we beg God
to explain himself, but instead he invites us
into those dark, inner spaces

where eternity is hidden—
in arroyos, caves, gorges, deep ravines—
to learn the virtue of emptiness.

Holy Thursday Pilgrimages
Chicago, March 26, 1959

We never made it to the seven churches
on those freezing Holy Thursday nights.

Spring may have sprouted on the calendar
but not tonight. This was no pilgrimage

to a humid Jerusalem upper room.
Here the drowsy street lights gave off

scant light and smoke struggled to escape
from the sagging bungalows and three-flats.

The neighborhood pilgrims who passed us
on the streets look as if they wore incense.

Every church we visited was dark except for the side
altars where there was an epiphany of light.

The noonday-bright monstrance was locked
as if Jesus were peacefully sleeping.

But the side altar was bursting with violet, purple,
and rose pink, all the colors of a lingering Lent.

The prayers of the faithful—processing in and
out—sounded like a weary organ. Jacob's angels but

no ladder anywhere to climb up to heaven.

The Capuchin Food Trucks

"Then he took the seven loaves and the fish, and when he had given thanks, he broke them and gave them to the disciples, and they in turn to the people. They all ate and were satisfied. Afterward the disciples picked up seven basketfuls of broken pieces that were left over. The number of those who ate was four thousand men, besides women and children."
—Matthew 15:36–38

On Tuesdays and Fridays they bring miracles
to the homeless multitudes who live on the rough edge,

under bridges, tucked into flea-lined
bedrolls, or over grates on soul-chilling nights.

The brown Capuchin Family Food Trucks,
St. Francis's face painted on the side, come to them.

The friars follow God's command, *"Bring them
to me,"* and load their traveling kitchens

to feed a crowd of mouths missing
teeth, futures, infected by despair.

The friars' hands like baskets are filled with
street manna—bread, warm, baked to share—

to nourish their brothers, the homeless
too often invisible.

But not to these friar cooks who have
packed their trucks with extra

portions, plates, plastic silverware,
even brown paper sacks to carry away

the leftovers. These trucks have helped
thousands feel the Holy Spirit in their gut.

Discipleship

In soup kitchens and shelters, they multiply
their fish and loaves. They bake hot cross buns
to feed the hungry on Good Friday and darn
the worn-out prayers of the homeless.

They tend flocks of children, abandoned
and abused, nurturing them with safe smiles
in the grim of night, protecting them
with millstones.

They pilgrimage to places where
the everlasting is rarely invited, prisons
with jailers' clinking hands, a drug trafficker's
corner, hissing in the dark abyss.

They bring the balm of salt and the charism
of sunsets to hospice-bedded souls
helping them mount the wings of eagles.
There is no absence in them.

A Woman Who Listened for the Lord

From the age of seven she slept with a Bible
under her head to hear God's word in her sleep.
At breakfast she quoted the Psalms.

At eighteen she married and took Proverbs 31
for her vows. She turned her heart into
a household for the wounded, the unwanted.

She spun her hair like flax and cut it
three times a year for wigs for women
struck bald by cancer's blows.

Her cabinets and freezer were treasuries
to support the poor; she drove miles
to bring them food from her house, far away.

She helped the blind to see holiness;
her lamp was never shaded. It cast light
on miracles, spittle turned into balm.

She was known for the heavenly clothes
she made for her family and the poor.
Local merchants swore angels sewed for her.

The Women's Shelter

The shelter is almost always full—
booked with running invitations because
a spouse battered so many commandments.

It is a hospice for the terrified of heart.
But the curtains on all the windows
are yellow even when the sun

doesn't shine and every room has a sky
blue prayer blanket, blessed, soft, signed
to keep bullies and assassins away.

But not the nightmares, threats, tears,
doubts, and *what ifs*. These last words are the welts
he planted in her conscience.

Shelter talk is less forgiving about
the past. Counselors ask abused women
how can a man stoke a fire in his chest

and not have his touch burn you and the children.
But his bone-breaking rage and molten anger
cannot flame and disfigure you here.

One abused woman knows she must go
on the other side of the padlocked gate tomorrow,
but she is traveling on a passport of prayers

and Bible verses to strengthen her self-worth.
She is not afraid of snow this winter.

In a Walmart Parking Lot

In the Walmart parking lot
a yellow spark mocks
the blessings of the stars. Going into
this dark emptiness, she processes down
corridors of cars repeating her five-second monologue:
"Pardon me, sir, I am homeless.
Can you spare a dollar." She sets her needs
low in expectation of something higher.
But President Washington won't buy her a meal.

The hostile silence of most shoppers
snarl pass her, thorns in their wallets.
This is not a landscape of charity.
Worse still are plaintiffs against her poverty
whose words stone her into further humiliation
caught in the act of seeking solace.

But rejection turns out to be
the other side of kindness when
a roundup customer reaches
into his conscience and gives her
a Hamiltonian feast at McDonald's.

Too few Walmart shoppers will ever receive
the Almoner's blessing.

Mother Teresa

You never abandoned anyone to the shadows
but gathered flocks of outcasts for the light—

they had less dignity than mud-
matted stones or flies on

decaying bodies. You cared for the dying
to give them the last rites of your comfort.

A beggar once asked you to put air
back into his lungs. Your smile

gave him the breath to bow before
God alive in you.

Your eyes glowed like cathedrals
solemnizing these untouchables,

seeing their sores and stringy
rags as scarlet vestments.

No one ever left your hospice
without a spiritual passport.

Your touch sent them higher
than the pyre smoke of Kolkata

which could never cloud the radiant faces
you saw in heaven's windows above.

Federico

You were a doctor, *Universidad
de Madrid*, *1950*, graduating
con altos honores, though

you chose Mother Teresa's
brand of medicine, taking care of
the least of these, the untouchables

who had no *pesos* or change of clothes.
You sought holiness by being one of them,
relieving their poverty of loneliness

by touching them in brotherhood.
Wealth for you was a millstone, fame
nothing more than a peacock's glitter.

When the *Sandinistas* came to take Christ
off the cross to interrogate him for insurrection,
you hid his wounded followers.

When you prayed for them your voice
was as quiet as a sunrise, your hands soft
as dove wings.

The Poor in Spirit

They have emptied themselves
of themselves. They feast on fasts
and find sustenance in humility.
What is good in them, they know
is God in them.

They see rainbows in lightning
and crops in failed fields.
They find paradise in caves
and hear God's voice in cloud weaves.
They do good for others,

then disappear. They carry wood
for monasteries, wash lepers' feet,
and bestow bread on the poor.
They care for orphans and widows.
At Easter they plant lilies everywhere.

They reject earthly pomp and wisdom.
They keep sparrows and look for
lost sheep on hillsides in winter mists.

If they have the keys to the Kingdom,
it is only to unlock doors for others.

Missionaries

They sail to places where their congregations
have never seen a map to plant churches
in jungles, deserts, in rainforests, in countries
not easily reached, and sometimes closed.

Calendars or clocks are unknown in some
of these places; time is measured in dreams
or animal migrations. Wildebeests or zebras
the timekeepers.

To communicate with their new flocks
they must learn to make sounds their ears
have never heard before. They teach
catechumens to recite God's name

in dialects without alphabets.
They sing in harmony with shafts
of sunlight; no sopranos here; only toucans,
hornbills, and parrots to take up the chorus.

They carry rainbows in their Bibles and build
ambries decorated with plantain leaves and
raise special praying bees for sanctuary candles.
Mists and moss help to teach spiritual lessons.

They know God's gathering places and where
to hunker down when storms, floods, or earth
slides threaten to overcome their will to believe.
They inscribe epitaphs on bamboo tombstones.

Unspoken Prayers
   St. Mark 7:31–37

Somewhere between our soil and God's sun,
between the puddles we drive through
and the ocean waves he tunes, somewhere

between flickering streetlights and the stars,
caves, and galaxies, the music of the spheres
and the half notes we play

we think we caught Christ, calling him away
from the immanence that surrounds him to heed
our cries and sew back the fabric of our lives

like some button on reason's foolscap.
We believe the fervor of our desires will gain
the favor he should crown us with.

Better to have baling wire wrapped tight
around our tongues to fence in our arrogance.
The best-said prayers are those unflourished,
unselfless, unscripted, unspoken.

Amen

It's not just tacked on at the end
of a prayer; it is a prayer itself.

Whether we read or shout
Amen, white space often follows

opening the sacred, taking
us into the beyond, the forever

Selah where we surrender our selves
to the light of *So be it*.

Inside this small word
a proclamation of faith.

Adam's first word rejoicing
in talking with God;

the fixed and firm profession
of the patriarchs;

the husband and wife's vows of
Forever and ever, Amen.

The *Amens* sung by a choir echoing
heaven's carillon.

A congregation receiving forgiveness
with amended hearts.

Life's Last Country

"Precious in the sight of the Lord is the death of his faithful servants."—Psalm 116:15

"There are only two days with fewer than twenty-four hours."—Kathryn Mannix, *With the End in Mind: Dying, Death, and Wisdom in the Age of Denial*

Ink

We are made of ink and into ink
we shall perish. Our history survives
in fire soot and boneblack pigment.

Carbon fingerprints tell our telling
and dust writes from dust.
Animal flesh enters the ink record.

Ochre and red flashes dart through
our quills. They humble our pride
in being able to script our voices alone

on papyrus, vellum, or paper.
Ink gyves our identities in gall
and gum. It gives us a life

and consigns us to death.
Registries say that once
we were here. But if ink fades

into wispy streaks or falls off
the page, our strokes and crosses
are lost and we go unmourned.

An Old Man Reflects on Job

I'm living a strange math.
A new year adds days to the calendar
but only subtracts them from mine.

I take shorter steps on longer distances.
My body is stamped with brown and red moles,
a dated passport to enter life's last country.

I carry an abundance of wrinkled leaves;
my friends are ghosts; my career ended;
my memory cannot be trusted

to translate the past; posterity refuses
to claim me, an orphan with a walker;
their hearts I once thought a refuge

from aloneness; but I am smoke
in their way fleeing from me;
all my paths have become extinct.

So many glossed lips once tolled love, home;
but all have found an elsewhere;
they muffle their words now and tint their eyes.

My thoughts are riddled with sores;
it hurts to think about a future.
Blowflies stalk me.

The Last Dwelling of the Flesh

Across from the nurse's station
at the hospice on Seventh Street,
the charts all read the same. No more
doses of time. No more X-rays, water,
IVs, shots, blood, tests, or doctors.

The last fragments of her body have
shrunk now by the pain that stripped
away muscles, arteries, smiles, words.
A shadow of herself lay beneath
those starchy white sheets.

As she rattles her last breath,
she sleeps in this world but dreams
in the next, a requiem and a homecoming.

Your Last COVID Words

We struggled to hear your last words but
in the thick dark everything sounds raspy.

Your voice acts as if it was suffocating,
strained through a virus-soaked quilt.

Were you pleading with us to stop the raw ice
from thrashing through your defenseless veins.

Did you think you were at old St. Aloysius's
confessing your forgotten sins to the priest.

Or were you whispering a goodbye, the last will
and testament of your life, letting us know

how much in just a few cracked syllables
we mean to you, bequeathing to us your memory.

But then silence intervened and a rubber sheet
smothered your exhausted words.

Shrouds Don't Have Pockets

"My grandmother used to say, 'Burial shrouds don't have pockets.'"
—Pope Francis, Palm Sunday, 2013

The Bible gives sound advice
about estate planning that
will benefit you here and

in the hereafter. First, use a bank
that will safeguard your soul's
assets in heaven where the books

are holy honest and your interest
never decreases. The best deposits—
tithing and supplying food and shelter

for the poor. These investments will be there
when Jesus asks for an account of your life.
Earthly treasure is eaten by moths,

gulped down by greed, and crumbles
to rust. It is counterfeit wealth and leads
to a ravenous depression.

Most of all, beware those with deep pockets
who have bankrupt hearts and shallow souls.
They forget that shrouds have no pockets.

Rain on the Pond

It's raining today
and the pond across
the street fills with tears

for so much pain
in the world. Scars
and scandals. Tombs

too early and forgiveness
too late, a funeral
for all those lost

in the forgetfulness
of time or the forgeries
of despair, abandoned

except for the prayer
circles our eyes say
for those we buried

and who come back
now, haloed,
grace on a gray day.

Lazarus Care

"I heard a loud voice... saying, 'Behold, God's dwelling is with the human race. He will dwell with them and they will be his people and God himself will always be with them as their God. He will wipe every tear from their eyes, and there shall be no more death or mourning, wailing or pain, for the old order has passed away.'"—Revelation 21:1–4

Francis's friars come today for those
who had no one to say their name
or bury their forgotten bodies.

They ready each one with dignity
to meet the light, their lost bodies
washed, anointed, celebrated.

Newborns are the hardest to bury
arriving from womb morgues
or massive steel cradles that rocked them
into trash, their lives lasting
only a few seconds.

No one has wept for them. But today
a volunteer family tearfully claims them.
Their coffins are so small.

Huddled among the nameless,
the homeless also have found a home,
a steel-made bed covered with a wooden cross
and a white blanket to keep the winter chill out.

Their lives were stolen by bottles, needles, smoke,
knives, bullets, despair. Starvation stripped them
into skeletons.

Others, too, come for burial: bloated suicides
dredged from rivers; immigrants
dying in crowded cells; abandoned seniors
in winter rooms, their broken chairs
stuffed into ovens for warmth.

Old St. Adalbert's Cemetery

*Developed in the late 1870s in Niles, Illinois,
a suburb just north of Chicago*

Even death dies here at old St. Adalbert's.
Rain and frost have wiped away the names
and dates from limestone grave markers
as ants and grasshoppers scratch their own
obituaries where once human ones stood.

Grave renters lost their squatter's rights
after a year if someone bought the plot
and simply pushed the renter down
with no record of who he or she was.

Lovers must bundle two feet and centuries
apart. Girls who once swung their cornsilk
hair and flashed quicksilver eyes can flirt now
only when rain dissolves their muddy bed curtains.

Wealthy souls bragged they could journey
into eternity above ground in Pullman-like
berths, but today moths tend their satin sheets—
their doors have not squeaked in a century.

The brown leaves of autumn flutter and
fall and are mistaken for sparrows
by the St. Adalbert dead hoping
God's eye has not forgotten them.

Walking toward Eternity

The monks at the Abbey of Gethsemani
avoid those cold stoney calling
cards to heaven. Those inscribed
with weeping angels, broken hearts,
or oak leaves overlooking locket-long
goodbyes with chiseled flowers. All for
corpses puffed up in finery and encased
in polished bronze, decorated bed chambers.

But lain between sheets of soil,
with only a cypress cross above,
the monks' bodies lie unadorned, hidden,
faces cowled and arms stripped
lest they enter eternity too worldly.

Their sandaled feet walk East.

Monroe's House

They removed the wooden ramp
with its mortised holes the day
the hospice nurse left. He heard
the pounding and hoped they'd use
the wood for his coffin. But he always
wanted to be a house. Or a part of one.

When his lungs gave out, so did the house.
They stripped it naked like a corpse, sold
the kitchen for scrap, and burned his clothes.
Then they removed the locks, the knobs, and
the doors, leaving nothing to be retrieved.
Still, his buried speech creeps into the walls,

and the floorboards creak a soft requiem.
The porch light continues to shine in the dark
the way his eyes did, and the grass sings
Irish green for him; feral animals continue
to graze on the timothy he scattered for them.
And the gatekeeper still keeps his name
on the roster of those who return home each night.

Monkey Grass
for Margie Parish

She planted monkey grass up and
down her steep driveway each spring;
it was her green menagerie.

Her plant-keeper outfit included a large
straw hat with swaths of sweat underneath
and fringe strings extending

out into the cloudless day surrounding her.
She joked the grass marked the border
between her house and heaven's gate.

It happily endured generations of kids'
bikes, drivers with their crushing
tires, and the scorching Mississippi sun

determined to wilt her monkeys.
But they survived many seasons
of blistering drought; they even stood

in a strong wind. But then she was gone,
and relatives forgot the monkeys; their drooping
crowns looked like frayed brown straw hats.

We Are Awaited

A train whistle rushes through a tunnel
filled with amber lights and low chants.

Sounds come from all directions;
but voices seem costumed to fit

the expectations I had for all those
whom I wanted to love me, but didn't.

I see them waiting on a platform
with used-up faces, their hearts

torn from their chests, falling
over their vests or sweaters.

Visions of houses I once lived in douse
my eyes, and a hand of fire writes my dates.

Then a conductor appears on the train
wearing a high hat, his mouth

filled with stones. His words
contain only vowels;

not a single consonant blurts out.
The train chuffs on until I lose

the weight of memory and my body
becomes soothing light.

About the Author

Philip C. Kolin is the Distinguished Professor of English Emeritus and Editor Emeritus of the *Southern Quarterly* at the University of Southern Mississippi. He has published over forty books on Shakespeare, Tennessee Williams, and African American playwrights including fifteen collections of poems. Among these are *Reading God's Handwriting* (Kaufmann Publishing, 2012); *Departures: Poems* (Negative Capability Press, 2014); *Reaching Forever: Poems* (Poiema Series, Cascade Books, 2019); *Delta Tears: Poems* (Main Street Rag, 2020); and *Americorona: Poems about the Pandemic* (Wipf and Stock, 2021). He has also published two books of poems about Civil Rights: *Emmett Till in Different States: Poems* (Third World Press, 2015) and *White Terror, Black Trauma: Resistance Poems about Black History* (Third World Press, 2023). And he has co-edited three anthologies of eco-poems on Katrina, the Mississippi River, and about the moon. His poems have appeared in *Agape, African American Review, America Magazine, Catholic Poetry Room, Christianity and Literature, Christian Century, Ekstasis, ISLE, Amethyst, Michigan Quarterly Review, Presence: A Journal of Catholic Poetry, St. Austin Review, St. Katherine Review, Spiritus, Sojourners, U.S. Catholic, The Windhover,* etc.